UK Benefits and Pensions 2025

A Comprehensive Guide to Understanding Pension Increases, Carer's Allowance Reforms, and Financial Support Adjustments

Ryan Sutton

Table of contents

Introduction: The Importance of Staying Informed on Benefits and Pension Increases

As living costs rise and the economic landscape changes, staying informed on updates to benefits and pensions is essential for millions of people across the UK. For pensioners, carers, and individuals relying on financial assistance, these adjustments directly impact day-to-day life and future financial security. The recent announcements by the Department for Work and Pensions (DWP) and government policies for 2025-26 reveal an increase in both pensions and benefits, designed to help support vulnerable groups during challenging times.

This book explores the significance of these updates, breaking down how various benefits—including state pensions, Carer's Allowance, and the annual Christmas Bonus—will change in the coming year. We'll look closely at how these modifications affect eligibility, payment amounts, and overall household finances. Additionally, we'll cover the DWP's new initiatives, such as anti-fraud measures and economic recovery programs, which aim to improve the sustainability of the welfare system while supporting those most in need.

Whether you're a pensioner, carer, or simply someone interested in understanding the future of the UK's welfare system, this guide offers a comprehensive look at the upcoming changes and what they mean for individuals and families nationwide. Through each chapter, we'll break down these updates to empower you with knowledge, allowing you to navigate these changes with confidence and clarity.

Chapter 1: Overview of the 2025-26 Benefit and Pension Adjustments

Detailed Overview

The 2025-26 adjustments to benefits and pensions reflect a strategic approach by the government to address both inflation and the specific needs of vulnerable groups. This chapter offers an in-depth exploration of the new rates, the rationale behind these changes, and their practical implications for recipients. While the adjustments apply broadly, their impact varies significantly between working-age individuals and pensioners, making this chapter essential for understanding how different demographics are affected.

Understanding the 1.7% Increase for Working-Age Benefits

The 1.7% increase in working-age benefits is based on the Consumer Price Index (CPI), intended to align benefit rates with current inflation. Although this increase aims to provide relief from rising costs, it has generated mixed reactions among recipients and policymakers alike.

Key points include:

Why 1.7%?

The government uses the CPI to determine adjustments, aiming to match cost-of-living increases. However, with recent inflationary pressures, many feel that the 1.7% increase may not adequately meet rising costs in essential areas such as food, energy, and housing.

- **Breakdown of Working-Age Benefits**

This section covers which benefits are included, such as Universal Credit, Housing Benefit, and Employment Support Allowance. Each benefit type is impacted differently depending on individual circumstances, making it essential for recipients to understand how the increase affects their specific benefit package.

- **Impact on Real Spending Power**

The real-world implications of a 1.7% increase on household budgets. For many recipients, the modest increase may only partially offset essential expenses, underscoring concerns over benefit adequacy amid high inflation.

The 4.1% State Pension Increase and What It Means for Pensioners

In contrast to working-age benefits, the state pension will see a significant 4.1% increase, in line with the government's commitment to the "triple lock" policy, which mandates that pensions grow annually by the highest of the three following metrics: 2.5%, wage growth, or inflation.

This section explores:

- **Triple Lock Policy Explained**

The triple lock has been in place to ensure pensions keep pace with inflation and wage growth, preventing a decline in pensioners' real spending power. This increase is expected to result in up to a £470 boost for over 12 million pensioners, a vital increase for those on a fixed income.

- ## How the Increase Impacts Pensioners' Financial Health

This increase aims to address financial insecurity among pensioners, many of whom rely on state pensions as their primary income. By enhancing their annual income, the government seeks to help cover rising expenses, particularly in energy and healthcare.

- ## Pensioner Poverty and Living Standards

The sufficiency of the state pension is still a worry in spite of the rise.This section briefly covers the prevalence of pensioner poverty, especially among older women and those without private pensions, and evaluates whether this increase will make a meaningful difference.

Final thought

The benefit and pension increases for 2025-26 reflect the government's approach to balancing limited resources with the needs of the UK's most vulnerable citizens. While the 1.7% CPI adjustment aims to address the rising costs of living for working-age individuals, the 4.1% pension increase underscores a commitment to protecting pensioners' financial health. This chapter provides readers with a thorough understanding of the motivations, impact, and controversies surrounding these changes, setting the stage for deeper exploration in subsequent chapters on eligibility, anti-fraud measures, and the long-term future of the UK welfare system.

Chapter 2: Understanding the Christmas Bonus

Overview

The annual Christmas Bonus is a one-off, tax-free payment that provides financial relief for individuals on certain benefits during the holiday season. This bonus, set at £10 since its inception in 1972, may seem modest by today's standards, but it remains a gesture aimed at helping those in need. This chapter explores the history, eligibility criteria, and practical impact of the Christmas Bonus, as well as why it has never been increased despite inflation.

The History and Purpose of the Christmas Bonus

The Christmas Bonus was introduced by Ted Heath's Conservative government in 1972 as a way to support low-income individuals and pensioners during the holiday period. At its launch, £10 held considerably more purchasing power than it does today, yet the payment amount has not been adjusted in over five decades. Here, we explore:

- **Initial Goals and Original Value**

When the bonus was first introduced, it was intended to provide meaningful holiday support, equivalent to around £165 today. This section explains why it was initially set at £10 and how its value has changed over the years.

- **Calls for Adjustment and Government Response**

Despite inflation eroding the bonus's value, there has been limited political momentum to increase the payment. This section covers discussions around updating the bonus to reflect modern costs and the reasons for its stagnation.

Eligibility Requirements for the Christmas Bonus

The Christmas Bonus is not automatically available to everyone on benefits. Eligibility is based on specific criteria, and only certain benefits qualify recipients for the payment. This section breaks down:

- **Who Qualifies for the Bonus**

To receive the bonus, individuals must be claiming one of several benefits during the "qualifying week," typically the first week of December. These benefits include State Pension, Personal Independence Payment (PIP), Attendance Allowance, Carer's Allowance, and more. This section provides a comprehensive list of qualifying benefits and explains who may or may not be eligible.

- **Qualifying Week and Payment Process**

The DWP determines eligibility based on residency and benefit status during the qualifying week, expected to fall in early December. This section details how the bonus is distributed, including how it appears on bank statements as "DWP XB."

The Impact of the Bonus and Public Perception

While the £10 bonus is a traditional gesture, its unchanged value has led to mixed public perceptions about its effectiveness. Here, we analyze:

- **Practical Impact on Recipients' Finances**

For many, £10 provides only a minor relief during a time of heightened expenses. This section explores how pensioners and low-income recipients view the bonus and how it factors into holiday spending.

- **Public and Political Sentiment**

Many argue that the Christmas Bonus should be increased to reflect inflation, while others view it as a symbolic gesture that still holds value. This section presents perspectives from public figures, advocacy groups, and recipients.

Final thought

The Christmas Bonus remains a hallmark of seasonal support for millions of Britons. Despite its modest value, it reflects the government's attempt to recognize the needs of pensioners and low-income individuals. As inflation continues to rise, however, the effectiveness and relevance of the bonus may come under further scrutiny. This chapter highlights how the bonus functions within the broader benefits system and sets the stage for discussions on whether similar benefits may see future adjustments.

Chapter 3: State Pension Increases and the Triple Lock Policy

Overview

The 4.1% increase in the state pension for 2025-26 represents the government's commitment to the "triple lock" policy, a mechanism that ensures pensions rise each year by the highest of three metrics: inflation, wage growth, or 2.5%. This chapter explores how the triple lock protects pensioner income, how the increase affects recipients, and why it remains a cornerstone of pension policy despite debates around its sustainability.

The Triple Lock Policy Explained

Since its introduction, the triple lock policy has been both praised and scrutinized. Here, we examine:

- **Origins and Purpose of the Triple Lock**

Introduced in 2010, the triple lock was designed to maintain pensioners' purchasing power, preventing declines in real income.

- **How It Works**

Each year, the state pension is increased by the highest of inflation, average wage growth, or 2.5%, ensuring pensioners' income adjusts to economic conditions.

- **Debates and Criticisms**

While the triple lock protects pensioners, some argue it is financially unsustainable, especially with rising inflation. This section covers ongoing debates and possible alternatives.

The 4.1% Pension Increase and Its Financial Impact

The 4.1% increase is anticipated to give more than 12 million retirees an additional £470 in 2025–2026. This section explores:

- **Who Benefits from the Increase**

Both the basic and new state pensions will see this 4.1% boost, with detailed breakdowns on how it impacts different types of pensions.

- **Financial Significance for Pensioners**

With the rising cost of essentials like energy and food, this increase offers some financial security. We'll examine how this aligns with pensioners' monthly expenses.

- **Long-Term Financial Projections**

Analyzing how this increase may affect pension costs in future budgets and what it means for the overall economy.

The Future of the Triple Lock

While the triple lock remains a key element of pension policy, its future is uncertain. Here, we explore:

- **Financial Sustainability**

As costs associated with the triple lock rise, there are concerns about its long-term viability.

This section examines projections and possible policy shifts.

- **Alternative Models and Proposals**

Various options have been proposed, including a "double lock" model or a set cap. This section reviews these alternatives and the potential impacts on pensioners.

Final thought

The 4.1% pension increase demonstrates the triple lock policy's strength in protecting pensioners against economic instability. As the government works to maintain this policy, debates around its future remain relevant. This chapter sheds light on why the triple lock is essential for pensioners and what challenges lie ahead in keeping it sustainable.

Chapter 3: State Pension Increases and the Triple Lock Policy

Overview

The 4.1% increase in the state pension for 2025-26 represents the government's commitment to the "triple lock" policy, a mechanism that ensures pensions rise each year by the highest of three metrics: inflation, wage growth, or 2.5%. This chapter explores how the triple lock protects pensioner income, how the increase affects recipients, and why it remains a cornerstone of pension policy despite debates around its sustainability.

The Triple Lock Policy Explained

Since its introduction, the triple lock policy has been both praised and scrutinized. Here, we examine:

- **Origins and Purpose of the Triple Lock**

Introduced in 2010, the triple lock was designed to maintain pensioners' purchasing power, preventing declines in real income.

- **How It Works**

Each year, the state pension is increased by the highest of inflation, average wage growth, or 2.5%, ensuring pensioners' income adjusts to economic conditions.

- **Debates and Criticisms**

While the triple lock protects pensioners, some argue it is financially unsustainable, especially with rising inflation. This section covers ongoing debates and possible alternatives.

The 4.1% Pension Increase and Its Financial Impact

The 4.1% increase is anticipated to give more than 12 million retirees an additional £470 in 2025–2026. This section explores:

- **Who Benefits from the Increase**

Both the basic and new state pensions will see this 4.1% boost, with detailed breakdowns on how it impacts different types of pensions.

- **Financial Significance for Pensioners**

With the rising cost of essentials like energy and food, this increase offers some financial security. We'll examine how this aligns with pensioners' monthly expenses.

- **Long-Term Financial Projections**

Analyzing how this increase may affect pension costs in future budgets and what it means for the overall economy.

The Future of the Triple Lock

While the triple lock remains a key element of pension policy, its future is uncertain. Here, we explore:

- **Financial Sustainability**

As costs associated with the triple lock rise, there are concerns about its long-term viability.

This section examines projections and possible policy shifts.

- **Alternative Models and Proposals**

Various options have been proposed, including a "double lock" model or a set cap. This section reviews these alternatives and the potential impacts on pensioners.

Final thought

The 4.1% pension increase demonstrates the triple lock policy's strength in protecting pensioners against economic instability. As the government works to maintain this policy, debates around its future remain relevant. This chapter sheds light on why the triple lock is essential for pensioners and what challenges lie ahead in keeping it sustainable.

Chapter 4: Working-Age Benefits and Cost of Living Adjustments

Overview

This chapter dives into the 1.7% increase for working-age benefits, an adjustment aligned with the Consumer Price Index (CPI). While this increase is intended to match inflation, rising living costs continue to strain many households. Here, we explore how this adjustment impacts those relying on benefits, whether it's adequate to cover essential expenses, and how it fits within the government's broader welfare strategy.

Breakdown of the 1.7% Increase for Working-Age Benefits

The 1.7% increase applies to various working-age benefits, such as Universal Credit, Housing Benefit, and Employment Support Allowance. This section covers:

- **Rationale for the CPI-Based Increase**

A look into why CPI is used to adjust benefit rates, aiming to match average cost-of-living increases.

- **Which Benefits Are Affected**

A detailed list of affected benefits and how the increase translates to monthly payments for recipients, depending on their benefit type.

How the Increase Impacts Household Finances

With high inflation affecting essentials like housing, utilities, and food, many argue that 1.7% may be insufficient for meeting rising costs. Here, we explore:

- **Expected Monthly Gains vs. Real Expenses**
Analyzing how the increase affects real spending power and whether it covers average household expenses.

- **Challenges for Vulnerable Groups**
A focus on specific challenges faced by low-income households, including single parents and those with disabilities, who often rely heavily on benefits.

Public Response and Future of Working-Age Benefits

The 1.7% increase has sparked diverse opinions among recipients, policymakers, and advocacy groups. In this section:

Reactions from Recipients and Advocacy Groups

Insights into the public's response, with quotes and viewpoints from people affected by the changes.

Potential for Future Adjustments

Discussion on whether the government might consider alternative adjustment methods or additional support, especially during times of high inflation.

Final thought

While the 1.7% increase aims to keep benefits aligned with CPI, many question whether it's enough to address the realities of rising living costs. This chapter highlights the importance of ongoing review and flexibility in welfare policies, especially as economic conditions shift. As we continue through the book, we'll explore other support measures and reforms aimed at tackling these financial pressures more effectively.

Chapter 5: Carer's Allowance and Upcoming Changes

Overview

Carer's Allowance offers essential financial support to those who dedicate time and effort to care for loved ones with disabilities. In the 2025-26 adjustments, the government will increase the earnings threshold for Carer's Allowance from £151 to £183 per week. This chapter explores the significance of this change, how it supports carers, and ongoing discussions around further reforms.

What Is Carer's Allowance and Who Qualifies?

Carer's Allowance is a benefit provided to individuals who spend at least 35 hours a week caring for someone receiving a qualifying disability benefit. Here, we look at:

- **Eligibility Requirements**

To qualify, carers must earn under the new limit of £183 weekly and meet other criteria, such as providing a specific number of weekly care hours.

- **Qualifying Disability Benefits**

List of benefits that qualify for Carer's Allowance, such as Personal Independence Payment (PIP) and Disability Living Allowance.

Impact of the Earnings Limit Increase

Increasing the earnings threshold for Carer's Allowance allows recipients to earn more while retaining eligibility. In this section, we explore:

How the £183 Limit Supports Carers' Financial Stability

With the increased threshold, carers can balance work with caregiving duties without risking their benefits, providing a vital financial boost.

Public and Expert Responses to the Change

Perspectives from advocacy groups and carers who welcome the adjustment and how they feel about the current structure of Carer's Allowance.

Future Considerations for Carer's Allowance

This section addresses discussions around potential future changes to the structure of Carer's Allowance, such as:

- **Calls for a Tapered Structure**

Many advocates argue that a "cliff-edge" cut-off penalizes carers who exceed the threshold by small amounts. A tapered structure could provide more flexible support.

- **Long-Term Goals for Carer Support**

Analysis of proposals for increasing Carer's Allowance payments, enhancing support for caregivers, and ensuring fair treatment for those providing essential care.

Final thought

The increase in Carer's Allowance earnings limit represents a positive step toward supporting carers financially. However, the chapter also highlights areas where future reforms could provide even greater support and flexibility. As the welfare system evolves, ongoing adjustments to benefits like Carer's Allowance can play a vital role in addressing the needs of those who care for loved ones.

Chapter 6: Eligibility Requirements for Benefits and Pension Payments

Overview

Understanding eligibility criteria for various benefits is essential, especially with new adjustments. This chapter details the qualifying conditions for major benefits, including state pensions, Carer's Allowance, and the Christmas Bonus. By clarifying residency requirements, benefit types, and age restrictions, this chapter helps recipients navigate eligibility and ensure they receive the support they're entitled to.

Key Eligibility Requirements for State Pension and Pension-Related Benefits

Eligibility for state pensions and associated benefits depends on several factors. Here, we explore:

- **Basic and New State Pension Eligibility**
Details on the age and contribution requirements to qualify for the basic and new state pensions, as well as spousal and survivor benefits.

- **Pension Credit Requirements**
Overview of the income-based criteria for Pension Credit, focusing on the guarantee element, which ensures a minimum income for pensioners.

Working-Age Benefit Eligibility

This section explains the requirements for popular working-age benefits, such as:

Universal Credit

Criteria based on age, income, residency, and family structure.

Disability Benefits

Eligibility guidelines for benefits like Personal Independence Payment (PIP) and Employment Support Allowance, focusing on health and income assessments.

Christmas Bonus and Residency Requirements

The Christmas Bonus has specific eligibility and residency rules. This section covers:

- **Who Receives the Christmas Bonus**

Eligibility criteria based on benefit type, residency status, and household situation.

- **Residency Rules for All Benefits**

Explanation of how living in the UK, the Channel Islands, or similar locations affects eligibility, and the implications for those temporarily outside the UK.

Final thought

Eligibility criteria can be complex, especially with overlapping requirements for different benefits. This chapter provides clarity on these guidelines, helping recipients confirm their qualification status and make the most of available support. As policies evolve, staying informed about these requirements is essential for those navigating the benefits system.

Chapter 7: Fraud Prevention and New Anti-Fraud Measures

Overview

To ensure that welfare support reaches those who truly need it, the government has introduced new anti-fraud measures. With billions lost each year to fraudulent claims, the Department for Work and Pensions (DWP) is implementing stricter controls and enhanced monitoring. This chapter explores the motivations behind these measures, how they work, and what they mean for claimants.

The Financial Impact of Fraud on the Welfare System

Fraudulent claims create significant strain on welfare resources, diverting funds from eligible individuals. This section covers:

Annual Costs of Fraud and Error

How much fraud costs the welfare system each year and its impact on budget allocations for legitimate claimants.

Motivations for Stricter Fraud Control

Understanding the government's focus on fraud reduction as a part of sustainable welfare management.

New Anti-Fraud Measures and Enforcement Techniques

The government's approach to fraud prevention includes enhanced technology and direct monitoring methods. Here, we explore:

- **Expanded DWP Counter-Fraud Teams**
Additional resources and personnel added to improve fraud detection and handling.

- **New Legal Powers**
Measures like direct access to bank accounts for debt recovery, which allow the DWP to monitor financial activity more effectively.

What This Means for Genuine Claimants

While targeting fraud, these measures aim to protect the welfare system's integrity. This section addresses:

- **Safeguards for Legitimate Recipients**

How the DWP ensures that genuine claimants are not unfairly impacted by these stricter controls.

- **Steps to Avoid Mistakes and Ensure Compliance**

Practical tips for recipients to avoid errors, stay informed, and communicate with the DWP to maintain compliance.

Final thought

The new anti-fraud measures represent a crucial step toward sustainable welfare management. By tackling fraud more aggressively, the government hopes to protect resources for eligible recipients while ensuring the system's integrity. This chapter highlights the balance between effective fraud prevention and fair treatment of genuine claimants, setting the stage for ongoing reforms in the welfare system.

Chapter 8: "Get Britain Working" White Paper and Economic Inactivity Initiatives

Overview

The "Get Britain Working" White Paper is a government initiative aimed at addressing economic inactivity and helping people re-enter the workforce. This chapter examines the White Paper's strategies, including targeted projects, cross-sector collaborations, and plans to reduce benefit dependency by promoting employment, education, and training opportunities.

The "Get Britain Working" White Paper's objectives

This section explores the White Paper's primary objectives, such as reducing long-term unemployment and addressing the root causes of economic inactivity. Key points include:

- **Addressing Skill Gaps**

Strategies for equipping individuals with the skills needed for today's job market.

- **Supporting the Most Vulnerable**

Specific focus on those at high risk of economic inactivity, including young people and long-term unemployed individuals.

Trailblazer Projects and Targeted Support

The White Paper introduces 16 new "trailblazer" projects to combat economic inactivity through practical, community-based initiatives. In this section, we look at:

- **Examples of Trailblazer Projects**

Case studies of projects aimed at specific groups, such as youth in education or individuals with disabilities.

- **Expected Impact on Local Communities**

How these initiatives are designed to create lasting change in local economies by helping individuals find meaningful employment.

Cross-Sector Collaboration and Integrated Approach

The White Paper emphasizes an integrated approach involving health, education, and welfare sectors to create sustainable solutions. Here, we explore:

- **Collaborations Across Departments**

How the DWP, NHS, and educational bodies work together to offer support that addresses both economic and social barriers.

- **Challenges and Potential for Long-Term Success**

Anticipated challenges in implementation, including budget constraints and the need for public support, as well as potential for lasting impact.

Final thought

The "Get Britain Working" White Paper represents a forward-thinking approach to economic inactivity, addressing the root causes with targeted projects and interdepartmental support. This chapter highlights how a coordinated strategy can help create sustainable pathways for employment, empowering individuals and communities across the UK.

Chapter 9: Looking Ahead – What to Expect in Future Budgets

Overview

As the government navigates economic challenges and demographic changes, welfare and benefit policies are likely to evolve. This chapter explores the future of UK benefits and pensions, analyzing how inflation, changing demographics, and economic conditions could shape future budgets. We also discuss possible adjustments to the triple lock policy, Carer's Allowance, and other benefits.

The Role of Economic Forecasts in Policy Decisions

Economic indicators such as inflation, wage growth, and unemployment rates play a key role in shaping benefits policy. This section covers:

- **Predicting Future Increases Based on Inflation and Wage Growth**

Analysis of recent trends and how they might influence future adjustments.

- **The Government's Long-Term Economic Goals**

How future policies may focus on reducing welfare dependency while supporting those most in need.

Potential Reforms to the Triple Lock and State Pension

The triple lock policy has protected pensions for over a decade, but its sustainability remains in question. Here, we explore:

Debates Around Adjusting or Replacing the Triple Lock
Possible shifts to a double lock or other modifications as a means of cost control.

Impacts of a Potential Reform on Pensioners
What changes to the triple lock could mean for future retirees and their financial security.

Evolving Support for Working-Age Benefits and Carer's Allowance

As cost of living challenges continue, future budgets may need to focus on improving support for working-age benefits and carers. This section covers:

Proposals for Expanded Carer's Support

Potential increases in Carer's Allowance payments and flexibility to meet the needs of today's carers.

Future of Cost of Living Adjustments

Discussions around how adjustments might better match actual expenses, especially in times of economic hardship.

Final thought

Future budgets will likely reflect a careful balance between fiscal responsibility and the need to support vulnerable populations. As inflation and economic demands shift, adjustments to benefits and pensions may become necessary to ensure both sustainability and adequate support. This chapter anticipates the changes that recipients may see in the years ahead, setting the stage for a dynamic welfare landscape in the UK.

Conclusion: Adapting to Changes in the UK Welfare System

Overview

The adjustments and reforms to the UK's benefits and pensions system reflect the government's ongoing efforts to balance economic sustainability with the financial needs of its citizens. From the annual increases in pensions and benefits to new measures addressing fraud and economic inactivity, these changes underscore the complexity of managing welfare policy in a fluctuating economy.

Reflecting on the 2025-26 Adjustments

The recent updates to benefits, including the 4.1% increase in pensions and the 1.7% increase in working-age benefits, reveal the government's commitment to providing relief for pensioners and vulnerable individuals amidst rising living costs. The introduction of expanded anti-fraud measures and the "Get Britain Working" initiative further illustrate how welfare policy must evolve to meet both fiscal demands and social responsibilities.

Embracing Change and Staying Informed

For those receiving benefits or pensions, understanding these adjustments—and staying aware of future updates—is essential. The impact of changes to eligibility, payment amounts, and anti-fraud policies can directly affect household budgets and financial planning. As these policies continue to evolve, recipients are encouraged to stay informed and utilize available resources to navigate the welfare system confidently.

Final Thoughts

The UK welfare system is at a critical juncture, with the government striving to balance support for vulnerable groups with the need for economic sustainability. As the welfare landscape changes, it remains vital for individuals to understand how new policies impact them and to adapt to these shifts. Whether you're a pensioner, a carer, or someone on working-age benefits, this book has aimed to equip you with the knowledge to navigate these changes effectively.

Thank You

Thank you for choosing this book as a resource to better understand the UK's benefits and pension updates. Your commitment to staying informed reflects your dedication to securing financial stability in a changing world. May this book serve as a valuable guide, helping you navigate today's welfare system with clarity and confidence.